"I devoured this collection. It is utterly brilliant. It h
many things. An amazing journey to read it cover t   it brings
back so much, viscerally, of Covid, lockdown, birth, babydom"

"Very witty, and relatable and honest"

"These poems speak to me and make me feel seen."

"I could read these words all day "

"Beautiful account of your introduction to motherhood."

"Susie has such a way with words and being able to bring the feeling to life just how it is."

Susanna Butt

Messy

Messy

Foreword

Messy is my debut poetry collection. It's the product of four years of journaling about motherhood, jotting down notes on my phone and hastily published poems on Instagram. The pandemic was where this poetry voyage began for me as I became locked in with my thoughts, locked into the house in my first year of being a new mother. Poetry became my friend, my outlet, my solace.

A friend introduced me to an amazing collective called The Mum Poem Press, a collective of poets writing and publishing poetry about motherhood. This was such a lifeline during lockdown. It's where I had my first poem published and how I started venturing into performing my poetry too.

I have always written but before having my daughter I mostly wrote lyrics to my songs. Not too dissimilar, it turns out, to writing poetry. But writing poems is just a little bit quieter and easy to navigate with a sleeping child in the room. Most of these poems were written whilst breastfeeding; sitting on a park bench whilst my daughter slept in her pram; or in the half light of the early hours of the morning.

They're an imperfect, messy collection of poems that I never would have dreamt of sharing so publicly. But, with encouragement, I kept going. Thank you to all of those who asked me to publish them and to keep sharing. These are for you.

'*Messy*' for me encapsulated the physical mess, the emotional mess, the fear of messing up, the non linear, constantly evolving messiness and imperfection of motherhood.

Thank you to Azalia for the beautiful illustration which captured so much of what I wanted to say. It's been a joy to work virtually with you on the design and I hope one day we will meet in real life!

Messy

Thank you Jess for firstly introducing me to the Mum Poem Press, what a lifeline, and for editing these before I put them out into the world. You are a star.

Thank you to Maya for inspiring me everyday, I hope one day I will inspire you too. Thank you to James for being my partner in crime and giving me space to write.

Messy

Messy	2
Foreword	3
Sleep Thief	7
Smells like motherhood	9
No Dignity	10
Co Sleeping	11
Leafy	12
Is anybody out there?	14
Two metres apart	16
2020	17
Lockdown Part II	20
One	23
I handed over a limb	26
Imposter	28
Boundaries	31
Messy	33
Earth Day	35
Absolutely Potty	37
Terrible twos	38
I am a Mother	40
Big Little Feelings	43
Is this normal	45
Three	47
Things I have learnt since becoming a parent	48

Messy

When	50
Fragile	52
Things I no longer spend money on	53
Where should we live?	55
Are we ready?	58
In my imagination	59
Power of connection	60
Enough	62
Day Dreamers	63
Four	64
I'm finding my way in the dark (song lyrics)	65
The carpet	67
Birds nest	68
Rush Hour	69
Mothering	71
About the Author	73

Messy

Sleep Thief

I never thought I could fall so in love
With someone who would steal my second true love
Before I had you I dreamed of sleep,
I slept the sleep,
I devoured the sleep,
I slept.

I was lucky to escape those dark bags creeping under eyes,
Eyes bright, eyes wide, eyes that had been closed for 8 hours straight.

The moment my waters broke, so too did my sleep.
Catapulted into a 36 hour labour
A new nocturnal behaviour
Sleep when they sleep
I'm repeatedly told
The reality of this is comedy gold
You the queen of the catnapper club
A record breaking 7 minute nap
Just time to pour the day saving cup of tea
I lay there with you next to me
Tug tug tug, suck suck suck
Trying to ninja out of your grasp
To steal some unobtainable time for me

I learn to hold the Kindle in one hand
Hiding behind your head,
I stealthily read as you sleep on me
A moment stolen for myself in bed
But you are no fool as you reach your hand behind
grabbing the object that's stolen my attention,
You aren't prepared to share
These precious moments of Mum and me
What happened to my self care?

Messy

Ten minute *Yoga with Adrienne*
Either you or the cat rolling all over the mat
Postnatal class in the park
Running to stop you eating the grass
or pulling the other babies' hair as they crawl past

I run the bath, it's ten past ten
Five minutes in a deep bubble soak
I hear down the monitor your wake-up croak

So marks the start of the night shift
The yo-yoing out of bed
For my little sleep thief is at it again
Stealing my youth and replacing with lines
Just one more chorus of '*You are my sunshine*'

When 6am rolls round
You wave at me as you are taken from our room
A morning walk with Dad, a victory for Mum
I steal one sleep back before breakfast time's begun.

Messy

Smells like motherhood

My embarrassment as the guests turned up early
I hadn't had a chance to shower
The secret no one dares share until you are part of the club
The postpartum smell has its own kind of power

I can still recall those distinct smells of the hospital
stiff starched sheets, anti-bacterial hand gel
The half tempting smell of stodgy baked potatoes
served after the ringing bell
Metallic smell of postpartum bleeding
The sugary syrup, luke warm watery tea
The sweet scent of body lotion to make me feel more like me

I breathe in the smell of your tiny head,
small enough to fit perfectly under mine.
The tropical sweet smell of your hair after bath time at six
The bath that washes away daytime spills of food, poo, milk and sick

The rich comforting smell of coffee in the morning
Now I am hooked on that quick fix
Fresh scent of blended courgette and mint
The weaning journey begins with the ubiquitous Joe Wicks

The faintly floral smell of the laundry
Strewn all over the house,
No more ideal homes aspirations
The lounge transformed into a launderette
The hand wash only items piled up in the sink
To add to the list of chores I often forget

Readjusted expectations, the releasing of control
Motherhood's filled my life with colour,
The joy of discovering things no matter how small
The comforting smell of you, the new familiar,
a life that was directionless now made whole.

Messy

No Dignity

When I became a mother
I lost my dignity
I lost my privacy
My deafening pregnancy snore
Peeing while laughing
Peeing while vomiting
Vomiting on the way to my first day at work

I lost my dignity
I lost my privacy
In labour in hospital
With my leg held in the air
As the surgeons cut me open and my partner saw right inside me
Wandering round the hospital in nothing but a backless robe
Wearing a giant nappy, peeing into a jug to show the nurse
The same nurse who inserted an enema into my backside

I lost my dignity
I lost any sense of privacy
Breastfeeding my baby on demand,
Accidentally flashing my breasts on the bus, in the park
Forgetting to put myself together again in public places
Until I noticed the expression on people's faces

I lost my dignity
I lost any sense of privacy
Talking about my intimate experiences with strangers in a baby class
I can no longer go to the loo without being followed
by my toddler, partner and cat
I never thought I would be as vulgar as that

I have gained many things since having a child
But I don't think I will ever. regain. my. dignity.

Messy

Co Sleeping

We managed six months with you in the next-to-me
I was fooled into thinking you were a sleeper with our 9-5am victory

Until the 4 month regression hit
I thought what's the fuss?
Then the night wakings began
and I began to feel like sh*t

An easy transition, to move you to the nursery
A big milestone on your six month anniversary
This is the beginning I thought, of you sleeping right through
If only I was right, but the reverse was true

The first night of protests
Caught me off guard
But I thought to myself this too shall pass
Spoke to the Health Visitor who told me this was normal
She'll take time to adjust to being on her own,
She's had six months of being in her womb-like home.

Ten months in, a year is passing too quick
We got sucked into co-sleeping
Believe me, this too will stick
At first it felt right
But soon began the sleepless nights
She wants to feed feed feed
She really gets on my tits
But I wake with her wrapped in my arms
and I feel like we are one
Sod the Baby Sleep Science book
God I love her to bits

Messy

Leafy

Taking walks together quickly became our routine
The joy of your face as I put you in the sling
You didn't want to be confined to your pram
With so much to explore and take in

You squealed with delight
Your little legs running through the air
At first you gripped my fingers tight
But once you had mastered it
You waved at everything in sight

In lockdown I looked forward to this highlight of our day
Long days cooped up inside
Looking for new ways to play
I wasn't sure how I would keep you entertained
Tried to think of new ideas
Buying new toys which were quickly cast aside

Little did I know that all it took
Was plucking a leaf off a tree
You carried it clenched in your little fist for miles and miles
As if you had caught the finest treasure
Your excited chuckle as I would pick a leaf for you to hold,
A different colour and shape
Puzzled at how to loosen your grip
Letting the leaf sail away like a feather

During the summer I carried the picnic mat in the pram
and would lay it under a tree
We would lie on the blanket, staring up at the sky
And watch the movements of the leaves
Casting shadows on our faces
As you began to crawl you would shuffle
towards the bushes inspecting these things
that waved at you in the wind,
Exploring through nature these mystical places.

Messy

It's autumn now and the leaves are falling all around us like confetti
The ground is a colourful carpet on which you will take your first few tentative steps
A whole year of walking with you through the seasons
Is something I will never forget

Soon you will have your very own tree
We will decorate at home
But these leaves are a little prickly
Like needles to touch
Dressed with twinkling lights
I can't wait to see your big blue eyes light up

It looks like the second wave is coming
But I am not so worried this time
Through your eyes there is much to explore.
I will kit us out in our warmest coats, hats and gloves
Ready to take on the enchanting outdoors.

Messy

Is anybody out there?

I wonder where you've all gone
disembodied voices
Whatsapp
Instagram
Voice notes
FaceTime
Zoom
We could be anywhere or nowhere
for seeing your face on a screen
is not the same as being seen
my daughter kisses faces on the laptop
we coo how cute
I worry what she makes of us
always on our screens
talking to 2D faces
She waves at strangers on the TV
are we all just characters in a show
walk-on parts
cameos
waiting for our big break
the raising of the curtain
the great big applause
as we walk out onto the stage
and the audience cheers
with anticipation for the show
to begin

Is anybody out there?
or have you all left
packed up and moved on

it's a year since I've seen
some of my oldest friends
we do our best to stay in touch
but some things have changed so much
babies have been born
friends fell in love

Messy

addresses have changed
friends have left the city, the country
returned from the other side of the world
but we could be anywhere or nowhere
when all that divides us now
is a screen

Is anybody out there?
or has my mind played a nasty trick
I scroll my social media feed
sometimes just to check
what you all look like
remind myself of your faces
but the pictures
that reflect back at me
could really be my own

here's us on a walk
or sitting working at home
we could be anywhere or nowhere
but at least we are not alone

Messy

Two metres apart

Three words that changed life as we knew it.
The distance between us stretches on and on
Metres turn to days, turn to weeks, turn to months
Two metres or an indefinite distance.

My daughter changes every day.
She smiles, a laugh, she rolls, 3 new hairs upon her head
Small moments become huge events that cannot be shared.

The presence of you, your spirit, your energy that fills a room,
Now a buffering image on a screen or a voice on the end of the phone.
An intangible distance.

I long for spontaneity, to sit next to a stranger, and chat about anything or nothing
Now I dance away from every encounter and view you with suspicion.

I want to walk into a room full of the people I love
Stand close enough to feel their breath on my face
and the music of their voices rising and falling and singing
Two metres divides us between then and now.

Messy

2020

The nights are long
The days are short
Everyone tells me it passes
in the blink of an eye
Lockdown made time
stand
still.

I don't want to wish away
I know our time
Together is short
Sometimes
I check the clock
Count the hours
Until your next nap
A chance to read, tidy, write, cook, shower, message a friend
Do
Nothing
I don't know what it was
I wanted to do
Without you

Those first 3 months
The hardest of all
Whirlwind
Nappy changes,
Feeds lasting all day
Racing to Urgent Care, the doctors or A&E
A rash on your face
A fall down the stairs
A blur of newborn anxiety

The next 6 months slowed right down
March brought the start of the lockdown
We were just getting into our pace
Planning trips and lunch dates

Messy

Quickly stolen away
The days felt endless
The sun was kind to keep shining through
As I spent most days outside with you

In July lockdown finally lifted
The diary quickly filled up
Desperate to see family
Meet my new niece
Get out of London
I crashed my friends car
Only minor
We were all in one piece
But the accident scared me
Left me feeling low
The responsibility
With a partner and baby in tow.

I felt invincible
After bringing a baby into the world
Like I could do anything
The accident shook me to my core
An absent-minded moment
An intrusive thought
What could have been
The kind nurse reassuring me
I'm doing my best
Mother to Mother
Making me feel seen

Lockdown lifted
Life began to return to normal
I went out for drinks with a couple of friends
Felt a bit of my old self return
Family visited
A longed for trip back home
Restored me
The joy of a home cooked meal
Making memories to store

Messy

To help the homesickness heal.

****

We are shut down again.
This time
I want to
Slow.
Right.
Down.
Relish.
The mess making
Rattle shaking
Nap taken on laps
Flap book page turning
Block building
Ball throwing
Phone stealing
Comfort feeding
Hair pulling
Finger pointing
Trolley pushing
Nursery rhyme singing
Mirror gazing
Moments
Of the time we have left
Before I return to the 9-5.

You will turn one on New Year's Eve
Born the last day of 2019
What a year it's been
The nights are long, the days are short
Stronger, wiser, more full of love
Look at how much together we've fought.

Messy

Lockdown Part II

Lockdown has descended upon us again
yet this time it feels different
less novel
that first lockdown
fear
a rush of activity,
toilet roll buying, frantic searching for online delivery,
queues around the corner
bursts of creativity
collective energy
sourdough baking
#stillgettingdressed
people trying to find their identity in the
anonymity of lockdown
Instagram lives, singing from balconies, Zoom parties,
the weekly applause
how do we stand out
reach out
connect with one another

The rush of anxiety
as I raced round the shopping aisles
The prickly heat creeping up my neck
Fearing that Covid was chasing me round the shop
Relief when I got back out into the open air
breathed
retreated
back to base

A life of rushing around
slowed right down
to these four walls
this street
four local parks and the cafes selling takeaway coffee.
I got to know our neighbours
we have a street WhatsApp

Messy

where the mundane and the trivial updates are shared
a sighting of a cat in a neighbour's house, a request for flour,
a new neighbour moving in, an old neighbour moving out
I have gone from living in a city to a village

A part of me was intrigued by the first lockdown
this new way of living
the unknown
the shared experience
living through something
that will make history

This time round there is a feeling of resignation
dark nights closing in
a collective sigh
a low hum of anxiety beneath the surface

Yet
we have learned to adapt
the self-conscious donning of a mask is now our daily uniform
I fall back into the routine of Zooms and online exercise classes
Happy Birthday sung out of time into the laptop
my daughter trying to reach into the screen at these familiar faces
obsessively applying hand gel until my hands are red raw
how long will it feel normal
not to hug each other
kiss each other
stop our babies from sharing their toys
with their playmates
no more play dates

I ventured into London the day before the second lockdown
the city felt far away
a stranger
a once familiar friend that had drifted away
I anxiously got on the train
feeling that I was rebelling
the once crowded streets emptying out
the quartet in Covent Garden playing to a handful of us

Messy

asking for tips as the plight of the musicians became dangerously real
expectant bars seeking people to fill the empty chairs thoughtfully distanced outside

I sat with my daughter alone in the Transport Museum cafe
one of the last ones to leave the city
the final countdown before
lockdown
this is London
but not how I knew it I wanted to tell her

A final hurrah before a month of
hibernation
focusing on the minutiae of the day to day
letting go of plans made
in haste and hope
wondering when we can plan with certainty again
an unsettling feeling of calm washing over me
as I find myself back in lockdown mode
nowhere to be
no time to be mindful of
and it all feels a bit too normal

Messy

One

One
whole year of you
One
day never the same, you grow, master new skills, always inquisitive
One
look at me, all the small acts of rebellion, forgotten

One
little miracle
One
positive test
One
minute to google 'predicted due date'
One
chance in 365 it is your dad's birthday
One
week after your due date you arrive on New Year's Eve
One
day before the end of twenty nineteen

One
little finger curled around mine
One
fine shock of dark hair down the middle of your tiny head, our little Mohican punk
One small brown birthmark on your lamb shank leg
One
time your name recorded as Maya Butt, in the hospital before you took your father's name

One
global pandemic, history in the making
One
long lockdown of stolen adventures
One

Messy

maternity year robbed of our freedoms but graced with the presence of mum and dad, the blessings of time

One
chance to get this right
One
long sleep to make it feel alright
One
date night, we threw down dinner, downed a glass of wine before you woke up, demanded we came home

One
you, only one you, don't try to be anyone else but you
One
me, only one of me, spread ever thinly trying to hold onto pieces of me to be the best of me for you

One
day I'll look back, how did I do it? Sleepless nights, 9 pregnant months, postpartum recovery, painful first feeds, dreaded trips to the loo
I would do it all again for another you
One
line across my womb to mark your dramatic entrance into this world
One
big meconium poo, I passed you to your father to clear up the goo

One
moment rolled into the next, desperately holding on to memories, they fall out of reach
One
love as big as the ocean
One
beating heart, I hope you can love me as you do now, for as long as I exist

One
month before you turn
One

Messy

big celebration on New Year's Eve, the party of all party nights, a
modest affair this year,
perhaps a glass of fizz over Zoom
One
large bottle of champagne to toast surviving
One
heck of a year
but the best of years
because of you.

Messy

I handed over a limb

I was dreading the day
I had to give you away
to a stranger
a qualified stranger
but a stranger nonetheless
if even for just a few hours a day
I felt I had just handed over a limb
as I left and walked the lonely walk home
feeling unnervingly weightless
without you weighing me down in the sling

You looked at me and screamed out "mama"
I tried to reassure you from the porch
but they quickly took you inside
and closed the door
like ripping off a plaster

it's better to say goodbye quickly
and try and reassure
with a confident smile
that I will be back
to pick you up in just a little while

I heard you cry on the other side of the door
a few steps down the road
I burst into tears
all the mixed emotions
guilt, worry, sadness, hope
the end of our year of us
the beginning of a new chapter
now a working mum
wearing lots of different hats
I will miss you
toddling around the house
always so busy
but I look forward to some adult chats

Messy

in my working hours
I feel a little bit jealous
of the time I won't get to spend
will you take your first few steps
or say your first few words
Will the childminder become your new best friend?

I look forward to our Fridays
Now our special day
I can spoil you with playing
and all the cuddles you want
make up for our lost time
I feel a bit more like me now
I get to use my brain
but you'll always be the highlight
of my day
my week
as I count the days
until it's Friday again.

Messy

Imposter

The new motherhood fog
my brain condensed to the essentials
of keeping a baby well and happy
reading '*Two shoes new shoes*' on repeat
living in the same clothes picked up off the floor
the daily wrestle of getting velcro shoes on your little feet

In no time at all I am back at work
sitting at our kitchen-dining-multipurpose table
still strewn with baby toys, a solitary sock,
specks of last nights catapulted dinner,
the permanent pile of laundry
hidden out of view
for the meetings over zoom

The house is quiet without you here
calm before your energetic storm
whirlwinds through the house
scattering the dust hiding in corners

My lunchbreak a little bit of luxury
exclusively me time
I can make a two course lunch
drink a warm cup of tea
go on a walking date with my other half
reminisce about a previous version of me

I'm relieved you are just up the road
I don't have the long commute back home
panicking I will be late
excusing myself from meetings
feeling that mother-worker-guilt

Since I returned to work
I have had to find

Messy

the 'other' me
the 'professional' me
rather than the 'mama' me
that taught you the word 'boo'
when your hands searched for milk

It's hard not to feel like an imposter
when I have been out of the game a while
In the year I have been gone
I have created and nurtured a wonderful human being
who can roar like a lion, moo like a cow,
waddle like a penguin, chuckle like a chimpanzee
sign for milk, the same sign for duck
and wield a spoon with wild abandon

Returning to work shouldn't seem such a big deal
after negotiating with a 12 month old
trying to teach the meaning of no
preventing accidents all day long
after being kept awake all night
finding the energy deep within me
to get creative and play
when all I feel like doing is having a nap, a shower
or dress for the day.

There are times I feel like an imposter
I have to quiet the voices
telling me I am not worthy of this job
If motherhood has taught me a thing
it is that I can achieve anything
and everything
and several things at once
while my body is still healing
and everything aches
and I'm hungry and tired
but propelled on by love
that no matter how intimidated I feel,

Messy

I have already made my biggest achievement
You are my life's work
I am just beginning
I will try my best
not to be
another
imposter
but a mother
and a boss.

Messy

Boundaries

Where do you end
and I begin
you started off inside me
now you sleep beside me
sometimes on me
attached to me
unable to sleep without me

I don't know how we got here
from breastfeeding to co-sleeping
to needing me through the night
I tried to wean, put you down to sleep
but you put up a mighty fight

A cry that could shake these four walls
you wouldn't take no for an answer
too weak willed
to stand up to your demands
I buried my head
in the sand
kept muddling through
this is not exactly what I had planned

I love how simple your needs are
unaware of societal convention
or judgment or looks
we are stiff upper lip, buttoned up
sort of people
you pull down my top
on the train, in the pool, in the pub
the most natural thing to you
comfort and food
my magic wand
Yet I feel embarrassed
at such a public display
of our private bond

Messy

I make excuses
for my choices
so personal to me,
to us
confused why it's anyone else's business
or why there is such a fuss
I'm just following your lead
relinquishing control
perhaps I'm lazy
or don't want a fight
As you grow more independent
there is an end in sight
to the constant need for cuddles
for being held tight

My boundaries are blurred
between you and I
where do you end
where do I begin
you are an extension of me
I will carry forever
like another limb

Messy

On my hands and knees wiping the splash mat again
wiping the thing intended for mess
so much time spent wiping
I'm beginning to care less about all the mess

Wiping the strands of hair stuck to your face
as you run your yogurt covered fingers through your once clean hair
wiping away the tears
as another tooth forces its way through
feeling helpless for the pain it causes you

Wiping the surfaces while trying to hold you
making your breakfast, feeding the cat
wiping the spilt water from the cat's bowl
after you tried to wash your hands in 'dat'

Wiping the sticky Calpol from the floor
after you fling the spoon out of my grasp
wiping the carpet after you've marched away,
your nappy hanging off, you sit back down on the carpet,
as I sit and watch somewhat aghast

Wiping the stains off the new sofa
the sofa that tells the tales
of baby reflux, meals fed to me whilst I fed you,
little hands smearing sticky marks,
each stain the marker of a new life lived in chaos

Wiping the sweat off my face
as I carry your now too heavy body in the sling,
after you refuse the pram
wiping the milk that has started to leak through my top
my weaning didn't go as planned

Wiping out those thoughts of the landfill I am causing

Messy

through countless nappies and wet wipes lying somewhere out of sight
those aspirations of being an eco mum
another thing to feel guilty about
but lack the time to make right

You take the wet wipes out of the packet and start wiping the surfaces and floors
amazing the things you pick up
when we make play from doing chores
I'll never quite catch up from the cleaning up after you
but perhaps you look around
and are disgusted by all the mess too

Earth Day

Dear Earth
thank you for letting me stay
on your wonderful planet
I know I'm only here a little while
in the bigger scheme of things
I hope when I leave you
I have done my best
to respect you
preserve you
and I've cleaned up all my mess

I apologise for my recent increase in waste
with nappies and wet wipes
thrown away meals not to my daughter's taste
I hope I can make up for the rubbish gone to landfill
by planting lots of trees
more flowers for the bees

Since lockdown began and the shops closed down
I have become a hunter of second hand goods,
reusing and recycling
swapping plastic toys for sustainable wood

A year of staying at home has made me see the impact of our travel
the air is much more clean
the sky a clear bright blue
wild animals wandered into cities
to discover what used to be their land
but the rush to return to normal
will see such things disband

I took for granted that I had all the time to explore
I've stayed local so long I am itching to see more
I will think twice about which car journeys I need to make
now I know how important it is to take care

Messy

to make sure your beauty can be shared
for our children and theirs and theirs

When the whole world closed its doors
and hid inside their homes
it was you that soothed me with your seasons
the reassuring cycles of life
the reliability of spring
and all the new life that brings

I saw life in its simplest form
I hope I never forget this time
when our worlds became so small
it made me realise what was important
and that I don't need it all.

Messy

Absolutely Potty

Poo poo, marvelous messy poo
On the carpet, the kitchen stool, in the bath, a wetsuit you gasp!
Total potty training books read… zero
Trying to be child-led by my potty mastering hero
You look at me so proudly after

Trips to the public loo, never thought I would
Relish these moments quite so much, holding your
Arms as you squat over the seat
"I did it" you squeal at anyone that will listen
Nappy free trip to the supermarket result
In a puddle on the floor
Not for the faint hearted this potty business
Getting there slowly…I smile as you say "I don't need you mummy"
and close the bathroom door.

Messy

Terrible twos

This chapter
is called
the terrible twos
a little unfair
but I can see how
we ended up there
raging tantrums
people stop and stare
screaming in the carrier
pulling my hair
rolling on the pavement
refusing the pushchair
I stand there
my patience waning
trying not to look
like I don't care

These fiery outbursts
push me to the edge
I want to cry from shame
of not being able to reason
or understand your demands
trying to assert whose boss
and show a sense of command

I know it's down to your frustration
there is always an explanation
If we make it home
without making a scene
I can't help feeling
a sense of elation

These terrible twos
leave us both confused
you don't want to put on your nappy,

Messy

clothes or shoes
sometimes you're overtired
constantly searching for clues
nothing worse than the screaming in public
or standing in queues

You little firecracker
I love your resolve,
a jigsaw puzzle mystery
I am trying to solve
you wise cracking character
don't ever get old

Keep pushing those boundaries
asking for more
I know you want to walk on your own
it's a tough world out there
I won't let you walk it alone

I fear how to keep you safe
you're already inching away
I know it's all about disrupting
learning through play
I'll try to give you the freedoms you crave
keep control when you misbehave
each of these stages are quick to pass
these wished away moments,
I'm already missing it
none of it lasts.

Messy

I am a Mother

I am a mother, yes
I am an individual too
I want to work hard, inspire, be a role model for you

I have dreams, desires and needs
as well as being the best mother to you
I want to carve a path for you to follow
in case you get lost in all the noise
so you can look up
see you can be whatever you want to be
ambitious dreams are not just for boys

They say history repeats itself
mistakes pass down the line
older generations had it harder than us
they couldn't have it all
things still aren't equal, but we live in a different time
since the days of giving everything up
to be a mother
I am a mother
to a daughter
the responsibility I feel is mine

When I grew up
we had a magnet on our fridge
"*To thine own self be true*"
who could be better than your own vision of you?
I hope you will see
I am a mother
and many other things too

We have more choices although we could do with more
we can try to juggle our jobs and be home for tea
we can have a more balanced life with supportive other halves
and some creativity
shared parental leave has made things more fair

Messy

but I reckon most mothers still do the lion's share

I learned as I've grown not to have regrets
not to lose all of yourself so you no longer know who you are
you will always be my longed for child
I am a mother
who had a mother
lost a mother
has a father
who became like a mother
found my mother again
when I became
a mother

I am a mother
when you grow up you might test me and drive me wild
but I don't own you and nor should I try
I want to nurture you and help you grow
until you are ready to fly

One day you will leave the nest
I will stand there proudly
as I watch you soar
over the hurdles of life
encouraging you to push for more
more than I had
more than my mother had
more than her mother had
more than her mother had
more for yourself and the daughters down the line
should you be as lucky as I

I will wait to welcome you back
always with an open door
ready to listen
not to judge or impose
advice from mothers is rarely listened to
as a daughter I know

Messy

I am a mother
I have lived a life before
have a lot of life still to live
I will always be there for you
but I can't just give give give
motherhood is a tug of war
between what we can and what we can't
I can only sow the seeds
help you grow
I am a mother
this much I know.

Messy

Big Little Feelings

I long to be as expressive
as a toddler
stamping my feet
folding my arms
throwing myself to the floor
screaming in public
squealing with excitement
dancing down the street
singing at the top of my voice
even if I don't know the words or the tune

They don't hold back in letting you know how they feel
showing you the intensity of their feelings
with the sheer force of their physicality
how uncomplicated
to live a world in black and white, yes or no, like or dislike.

When I'm sad I often hide it
who then will comfort me?

When I'm angry I bottle it up
carry it around like a heavy beast
as it threatens to burst through the seams

When I'm happy I play it down
afraid happiness may fall out of reach

Somewhere along the line I stopped expressing myself freely with unabandoned joy
started to hide the parts of me that wanted to break free,
the storyteller, the singer, the traveller, the maker of stories,
the child that had big dreams and no boundaries.

I started to believe daydreaming was a weakness
I forgot how to let my mind just sit and wander,

Messy

wander into new worlds

What if I had never stopped.
daydreaming
dreaming
playing
saying exactly what I meant
showing exactly how I felt.

The time I might have saved
the things I might have made
the stories I might have told
I yearn to be young and fearless
to age, yes,
but never grow old.

Is this normal

Is this
normal
Am I
normal
Is she
normal
Are we
normal
How long is
normal
How much is
normal
Does this look
normal
Is this phase
normal
Is that cry
normal
Is that mark
normal
Is that behaviour
normal
Is this pain
normal
Is bed sharing
normal
Is this fear
normal
Is this feeling
normal
Is this sadness
normal
Is this tiredness
normal
Is this question
normal

Messy

What is normal?

Messy

Three

Three years of growing, learning and knowing you
Working out my identity as you take small steps away from me
Three words encapsulate my feelings for you
Three is the magic number but perhaps one day we will be more
Three things I love about you
Your giggle, head-locking hugs, wet nosed kisses
I couldn't love you more
Three turns around the sun
You are the ray of light when darkness falls
Three going on thirteen
You outwit and surprise me with your observations
Already commanding yourself like a queen
3-2-1 you've only just begun
On your incredible journey
I am so grateful to share with you, little one.

Messy

Things I have learnt since becoming a parent

I am a contortionist
fitting into small spaces
pulling silly faces
winning "mummy be a cat" races

I am a driver to all the different places
toddler groups, play dates, grandparents, holidays
entertainer, making up songs about things I see on the road
passing you snacks so you don't explode

I am an intrepid explorer
teaching you how to find Gruffalo in the woods
or the big bad mouse
leading the search for Winnie the Pooh's house

I am a chef to the most hard to please
whipping up smoothies and the macaroni without cheese

I am the packer of bags
the provider of snacks
the public loo location scout
ready to race as soon as you shout
I need a weeeeee
the time keeping wizard
knowing when hunger will strike
I have muscular arms that can carry a child and a bike

I am the masseuse and the healer
"No mummy do it like this"
the actress and the reader
the singer and the leader

The project manager

Messy

failing every day to leave on time
the negotiator and the diplomat
"If you leave the house now you can wear that ridiculous hat."
the peace keeper and protector of the most tormented cat

The risk assessor
first aider
lollipop lady
anticipating every possible hazard and fall
the frugality expert
surviving on £500 a month
learning how not to have it all

The night owl watching over you
as you sleep & wake & sleep & wake
lying next to you in your tiny bed
until all of me aches.

Messy

When

When will I stop wanting
will I ever have enough
seeking that temporary rush
from accumulating stuff

When will I stop comparing
will I ever be enough
consumed by rolling highlights
blinded to the lows
no life is perfect
I worked hard
for the path I chose

There were many paths
I could have taken
the one I took led me here
If I could change one thing
I wouldn't
the cost would be too dear

When will I stop wishing
time moved fast,
stayed still
If this moment is all I had
would I waste it wanting
being present
is an admirable skill

Every second I spend
of my precious time
gazing at other's lives
is a second I have lost
of living in mine.

When will I stop worrying

Messy

about the things I don't have
I am rich with the things I do
when will I stop wanting
all I wanted was you.

Messy

Fragile

Our minds are fragile, fragile like dust
the more we hide, the more that is lost
a neglected bicycle will sit and rust

Our thoughts can be the undoing of us
round and round, in circles we go
our minds are fragile, fragile like dust

We're taught not to make a fuss
a memory, flashback, trauma, trigger,
the punctures in the tyres will only get bigger
a neglected bicycle will sit and rust

I wish I could unburden you, convince you to trust
our histories and experiences don't define us,
our minds are fragile, fragile like dust

Was it a different life, the thing that you lust
are their regrets you haven't discussed
our minds are fragile, fragile like dust
a neglected bicycle will sit and rust

Things I no longer spend money on

Professional wax
far too lax
hair colouring
no time to relax
high heels
comfort and speed is what I need
dry clean only clothes
can't afford with rising household bills
white clothes
camouflage or dark colours to disguise the spills
fancy underwear
still rocking my giant hospital pants
foreign holidays
a distant memory
Ubers
I barely go out
make up
maybe a spot of lipstick for my insta perfect pout
pretty house furnishings
mostly throws to disguise the stains
quality brand toiletries
budget home brands much to my disdain
brunch
All day breakfast? I'm lucky if I get to sit down to eat lunch

Things I spend my money on

Coffee
coffee
coffee
caffeine is king
gin

Messy

mother's ruin but count me in
babyccinos
milk
overpriced baby snacks
raisins, blueberries, bananas
never seem to have time to make flapjack
leggings
flexible wear is where it's at
childcare (costs as much as the mortgage)
sky high mortgage for a house not much bigger than a flat
storage
so many toys and pointless tat
cleaning products
washing powder
the constant washing, no end in sight
nappies
wet wipes
cotton wool
my personal contribution to the planet's plight
baby bath products
certain product's a rip off, I prefer the spin-offs
toddler clothes replaced every few months
toddler shoes replaced every few months
anything with wheels on

waiting for me to trip
anything with dinosaurs on
stickers do the trick
hair clips lost daily
they really never stick
soft play
the only way to spend a rainy day
ice cream
*my no sugar rule weakens as you scream
I want ice cream!!*

Messy

Where should we live?

Tired of London
tired of life
Samuel Johnson said
Where should we live?
the thought that keeps me awake in bed

With a toddler in tow
priorities quickly change
"You need more space, a garden, a garage,
a bigger fridge, airing cupboard, a kitchen range"

Two up, two down
felt like a generous space
after sharing a one bedroom flat
now we have a toddler, house plants, and a cat
There's a park across the road with slides, splash pool,
climbing frame and swings
but since we've had a toddler
our house is full of things
trip hazards everywhere
laundry in the lounge
small toy hoover, a wheely-bug mouse,
pushchair, toy box, trolley, pram
how much can we cram
in our small but beloved house

Do we move to the country
to get more space
but what would we do there
would we disappear without a trace?
Would people come and visit
or would we live near friends
or live near our family
welcome the help they might lend

Messy

What of our jobs
and a longer commute
and the extra expense
so much to compute

Do we stay where we are
a journey too far
for our families to pop in
do we make the big move
leave our frantic city lives
with everything on our doorstep
finances stretched to the max
do we jack it all in
for a quieter life
Three bed house with a garden
and space to relax

How do you make the decision
when is it the right time to go?
It's hard to come back once you leave
so when we go, we go
So much to do in the city,
parks, culture, theatre, bright lights,
a magical place
Would it be better
to leave the rat race?

Am I ready to grow up
leave dreams in the city
is it selfish to stay
where pollution is rife
busy roads, my daily fear
cost of living sky high

I want what is best
for you, for us,
to not go without
Is there ever a wrong choice

Messy

or a life without doubt
the most important thing
is a roof over your head
a house full of love

We don't need the things
the space or the excess cash
Only food, fun, play, time together,
not a life with all the trimmings,
a life too showy or too flash.

Messy

Are we ready?

Are we ready to go from three to four
because naturally I always want more
all around us friends are becoming four, five
and life is such a race and I feel like I need to keep up
the clock is ticking, fast
you are growing up
I'm already mourning the past
looking back at photos and videos of you as a baby, your first smile, word, stumble,
I ache to live it all again
just as the chaos begins to mellow
we are in our little groove
you still need me and I you
desperately trying to carve out time for me and you
between the work and the chores and the friends and the logistics
are we enough for you?
If three becomes four will the boat start to sink
is it possible to overthink
bringing another human into the world
I grew up with 3 siblings
they are my tribe
whenever I feel lost
I have my tribe
they know me more than anyone
how lucky I am
to have my tribe
I want that for you
but when we are ready
when you are ready
when my body is ready
if it's not too late

Messy

In my imagination

I'm building an extension
in my imagination
so my mind can travel freely
with plenty of room to explore
I'm going to knock down the walls
and take out all the doors
that keep me safe and stop me running from my fears
I'm putting in a skylight
to let in all the daylight
so I never sit alone in the dark
I want an island in the middle
to escape to from time to time
and an extra room for storage
for my never ending thoughts

Messy

Power of connection

Sunflower seeds
sent in the post from my sister to my daughter
reach their eager heads towards the sky
I show them to you
retelling how we planted them together
you and I

Blossom falls from the trees
I pick the pink confetti from the ground
placing it in your hand
to teach you about the seasons
as every season passes
you unfurl,
your limbs growing sturdier,
your arms reaching out
like branches unsteady in the wind,
your hair losing those first few curls

Daffodils I potted last spring
rise up again
spill yellow sunshine
onto the courtyard
reminding me of the cycle of things

Courgette seeds
potted at Grandma's house
lovingly watered with your toy watering can
after years of separation
we sow seeds
from which we will grow new life once again

The rose I repotted from my birthday
gifted from my father to me
grew buds the colour of happiness
memories of family gatherings
as I celebrate another year

Messy

another chance to bloom wherever I am planted,
grow new life,
and turn my head towards the sun.

Messy

Enough

I am enough
I do enough
I try enough

I've had enough
of feeling like I am not
enough
of feeling like I could do more
earn more
exercise more
parent more
work more
clean more
socialise more
call more
save more
plan more
play more
smile more
floss more
travel more

there's always more

sometimes more is not enough
more is limitless
I am not limitless
I have my limits
because I am
enough.

Messy

Day Dreamers

Sometimes I stay in your bed while you've fallen asleep to
daydream
I offer to drive to the dump so I can sit there
daydream
sometimes it's about the other career I dream of having
accepting my Oscar or my Grammy or both
lying scantily clad on a beach
cycling with my feet off the pedals and the wind rushing through my
hair
I'm browsing market stalls in a hot country buying bowls I do not
need that won't get broken as soon as I bring them home
I wonder if I should
daydream
if I'm allowed to
daydream
why I
daydream.
perhaps it's me rebelling against the domestic drudgery
perhaps I haven't let my hair down in a while
you'd probably think I'm mad if I told you my daydreams
but they are my little secret island
and no one's invited.

Messy

Four

Force of nature, forever in
Orbit, my whole
Universe, shining proudly like a star
Reminding me every day, born of the same DNA, how similar we are.

Messy

I'm finding my way in the dark (*song lyrics*)

I'm finding my way in the dark
we're awake with the larks
is there anyone out there
who can teach me
the parent I want to be
because I find it hard to ask
and I don't know who to ask

to make sure I'm getting it right
sometimes I feel alone in the night
even though I'm lying next to you
I'm scared by how much you need me
how much you'll need me
and how much I'll need you

I'm finding my way in the dark
I've lost my way on my path
will I ever find my way back
find my way back
in the dark

I was looking for a hand to hold
I wanted a hand to hold mine
while I held yours
I wanted someone to hold me
while I was holding you
I wanted a hand to lead me
while I was lost in the dark

I'm coming out into the light
I knew somehow we'd be alright
we made up our own path

Messy

and our own rules
and now you're ready to start school

I found my way in the dark
You are my joy and my spark
I stay by your side until you drift off to sleep
I'm there when you wake with the larks.

Messy

The carpet

I can't seem to sit still
settle like dust
free falling
I can't seem to get comfortable
I seem to avoid things that will bring me comfort
I sabotage success
run from a helping hand
I wonder why I don't allow myself to become
who I am meant to be
what am I afraid of
I'm afraid.
I once heard
if the carpet has been pulled from under you
that you never stand still
you have to keep moving
knowing that the earth beneath your feet
is constantly shifting
I live moment to moment
inches from the edge
always alert
a bag never fully unpacked
I keep my armour on
I keep on keeping on
never standing still
never getting comfortable
flying the carpet
but never quite ready
to land.

Messy

Birds nest

You were too young to flee the nest
camouflaged against the branches
and the feathers woven with love
you were still a chick
learning to fly without knowing if someone will catch you.
taking your first leap without
a guide to take you under their wing
knowing that when you land
predators were waiting in the shadows
and protectors were hiding in their own
you were searching for love
and only finding breadcrumbs
your heart hungry
your belly full of fire
your wings clipped
your mind aflame with desire.

Messy

Rush Hour

I hate being rushed
I am a bull
stubborn slow and strong
I like to plod along at my own sweet pace
I wonder why sometimes I feel behind
why I still feel like a penniless student
driving an ancient car
looking back on the last ten years
it seems I haven't moved all that far

I'm not high flying
or mothering a family of five
moving from house to house in search of something better
ticking off countries on the map
I haven't run that marathon
 written my first book
made an album
It's not because I'm lazy

I just don't like being in a rush
I like to take my time
notice all that's lush
I like to walk more than drive
I like chatting to my daughter in bed in the morning
listening to her talk about her day until she falls asleep
I like to read books, re-reading pages at a time
I like to eat my food slow, one mouthful at a time
I like to stop and talk to a friend I bump into on the street, ask them
how they are
I like to sit on the train and stare out the window
I don't mind if it's late as I get to think some more
The only thing is
I hope I live to 100
because I want to take my time
to savour all that is good
every moment in time

Messy

I know I'm supposed to be in the rush hour of life
but I don't want to rush it at all.

Messy

Mothering

Becoming a mother has been like peeling away the layers of me one by one
raw
wild
naked.
I have been blinded by love but also grief
Grief for the lost maternal years,
I have never felt so alive yet so closed off to the world
So full of love, so desperately craving maternal love.

Mothering
It's not just mothering a child.
Mothering is nurturing, protecting, caring for others
I am fortunate to have been mothered by so many, my mother, my father, my friends and family.
To have picked up the loose threads of my own maternal tapestry and woven our relationship back into the story stitch by stitch

Raising a person does take a village
If one of us falls or falters we need someone to step up, step in.
Our lives have become less connected, fragments spread across cities, across the country
We are more connected by technology
But that means nothing when
You can't be physically here to hold

They say trauma can pass down the generations
Through our roots, our bloodlines, our DNA
It can be felt many years down the line.
The things that change us, haunt us can be passed on.
But we can heal
We can change the course of history
By understanding, listening, compassion
Not carrying the burden of hurt or blame or family secrets.

Messy

Each generation we have the chance to start again if we are open to change and allow ourselves to be vulnerable.

**

Your arrival into this world was not picture perfect
It was the start of a perfect storm
I spent many nights lying with you in the dark
I struggled with routine and formulas
pick up put down, scheduling of naps
I was totally led by you, by biology, following your rhythms and your cues. Every nap a contact nap, I barely put you down.
I gave up on all the books, all the apps and listened only to you.
You showed me and I followed and we found our way in the end.

My version of motherhood may be a bit messy

I don't always have it under control

I don't have a plan or know what's happening the week after next

I can't afford many of the things we seem to need to have

I worry constantly how I'll make it all work

but that doesn't mean I'm not doing it right.

I'm doing my best

I may make a mess

Sometimes the best works of art

are the ones where we were brave enough to draw outside of the lines.

When we allow ourselves to be messy, we allow others to be messy too.

Messy

About the Author

Susie is a singer, songwriter, poet, arts fundraiser and Mum to Maya living in Beckenham, Kent. This is her first poetry collection. Susie has had two poems published in the Mum Poem Press publications, "Songs of Love and Strength" and "The Mum Poet Club guide to Self Care."

She has performed as a poet with the Mum Poem Press at "Book the Babysitter" at Soho Theatre and at the Tunbridge Wells Poetry Festival.

As a songwriter she has self released 3 EPs, "Promise me" "So This is our Dance" and "Still I Rise".

X: @susiebmusic
Instagram: @susiebmusic
www.susiebmusic.com